Fun Ways to Learn the Whole Story of Jesus and His Love

Jesus Works Miracles

Creative Bible-Learning Activities for Children Ages 6-12

The buyer of this book may reproduce pages for classroom and home use.
Duplication for any other use is prohibited without written permission from David C. Cook Publishing Co.

Copyright © 1991 by Tracy Leffingwell Harrast. All rights reserved.
Published by David C. Cook Church Ministry Resources, a division of Cook Communications Ministries International.
Printed in the United States of America.

All puzzles and Bible activities are based on the NIV.

Scripture taken from the Holy Bible, New International Version, Copyright © 1973,
1978, 1984 International Bible Society.
Used by permission of Zondervan Bible Publishers.

Book Design by Tabb Associates
Cover Illustration by Gary Locke
Interior Illustration by Anne Kennedy

10 9 8 7 6 5 4

THIS BOOK BELONGS TO:

_____

To My Children and Others Who Read This Book

When you're afraid, remember how Jesus calmed the storm. Just as He made the wind and sea calm and rescued His disciples, He can give you peace when you're afraid. When you feel things are hopeless and as if nothing can help you, remember the miracles Jesus worked while He was on the earth. Nothing is too big for the Lord to handle. You can trust Him to answer your prayers—He has the power to do so.

—Tracy L. Harrast

Jesus Works Miracles
CONTENTS

Palestine, Where Jesus Lived 5

Miracles Are A-maze-ing 6

Miracle Matchup 7

Jesus Changes Water to Wine (John 2:1-11) 8

Jesus' First Miracle 9-10

Jesus Fills the Net (Luke 5:3-11) 11

Become a "Fisher of Men" 12-13

Make a Sponge Fish 14

Make a Boat (Matthew 8:23-27; Mark 4:35-41; Luke 8:22-25) 15

Caught in a Storm 16-17

Tossed About in the Storm 18

See the Sea 19

The Missing Word 20

A Puzzling Story 21

Rely on God 22-23

Jesus Feeds Thousands of People (Matthew 14:15-21; 15:32-38; Mark 6:33-44; 8:1-9;
   Luke 9:11-17; John 6:5-15) 24

My "Loaves and Fish" 25

Make a Diorama 26-27

Jesus Walks on Water (Matthew 14:22, 23; Mark 6:45-52; John 6:17-21) 28-29

Would Your Faith Sink or Float? 30

Faith to Float 31

Make a String Picture 32-33

The Coin in a Fish's Mouth (Matthew 17:24-27) 35

Jesus Withers a Fig Tree (Matthew 21:18-22; Mark 11:12-14, 20-26) 36-37

Jesus Fills the Nets Again! (John 21:1-24) 38

Play a Fishing Game 39
Answers 41-42
I DID IT! 43
Index of Series 44-45
Write the Author 46

Palestine, Where Jesus Lived

Draw a line from each miracle to the place where Jesus worked it.

1. Jesus changes water to wine at a wedding in Cana.
2. Jesus fills a net with fish at the Sea of Galilee.
3. Jesus calms a storm on the Sea of Galilee.
4. Jesus feeds thousands at Bethsaida.
5. Jesus feeds thousands at a mountain near the Sea of Galilee.
6. Jesus walks on the Sea of Galilee.
7. While in Capernaum, Jesus sends Peter to find a coin in a fish's mouth.
8. Jesus makes a fig tree wither in Bethany.

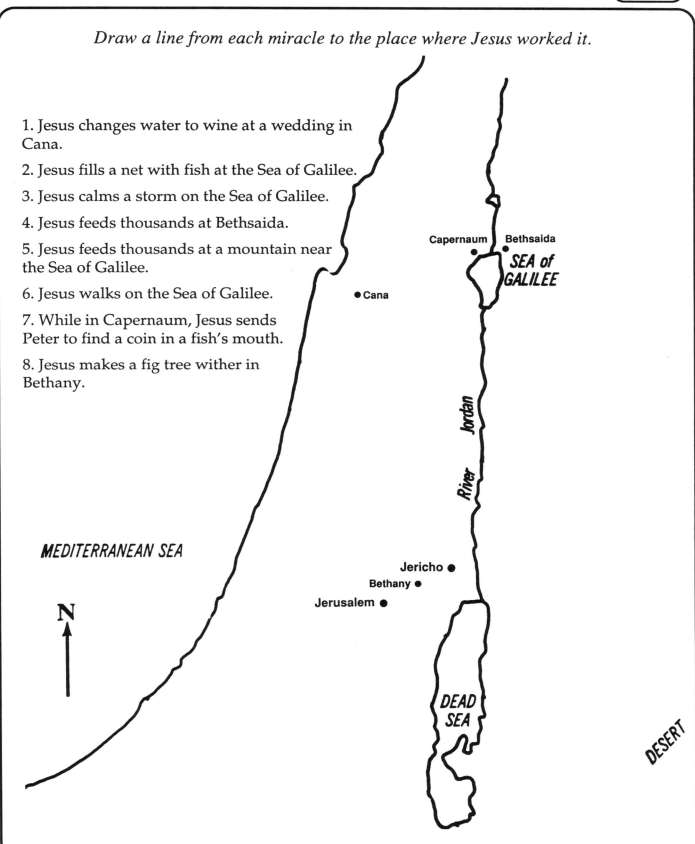

Miracles Are A-maze-ing

Answer these questions and then see if your answers are right by using them to direct you through the maze. If they're correct, you'll go from the beginning to the end without getting stuck.

1. Are miracles real?
2. Is a miracle a trick?
3. Are miracles supposed to entertain?
4. Do miracles help people's faith in God become stronger?
5. Is it possible for miracles to happen today?
6. Are miracles done with magic?
7. Is the greatest miracle that Jesus rose from the dead so we can live forever with God?

START **FINISH**

Miracle Matchup

Put the letter of each miracle under the picture it matches.

A. Jesus turns water to wine
B. Jesus fills a net with fish
C. Jesus calms a storm
D. Jesus feeds thousands from five loaves and two fish
E. Jesus walks on the sea
F. Jesus knows a coin will be in a fish's mouth

Jesus Changes Water to Wine

When you come to a scrambled word in the story, unscramble it and write in the correct word. This way you can read about Jesus' first miracle.

One day Jesus, His disciples (followers), and his **hmtore** _____ (Mary) attended a **wgednid** _____. After a while, the host ran out of **inwe** _____, and Mary told Jesus. Jesus **kesda** _____ what Mary wanted Him to do. Mary didn't **sawnre** _____, but she told the servants to do whatever Jesus told **meth** _____ to do.

There were six **eotns** _____ water pots there, which could hold **wnttye** _____ or thirty gallons each. Jesus said to **lilf** _____ the pots with **rawet** _____, and the servants did. Jesus then told one of the servants to give **eosm** _____ to the host of the wedding **sefat** _____.

The wedding host didn't believe the wine he tasted had once been water. He said he was happily surprised that the groom had **vased** _____ the best wine for last.

Jesus did this first **rimcale** _____ in Cana of Galilee and His disciples believed that He was God's Son.

Draw a star in this box when you've read the story in John 2:1-11.

Jesus' First Miracle

Jesus

Disciples

Mary

Wedding Host

Servant

Servant

Color these characters from the first miracle Jesus worked. Then cut out the figures, and tape them to spoons to make puppets.

Put on a puppet show for your family and friends in which puppets perform the story of Jesus changing the water into wine. For a special effect, you might want to pour a grape drink mix into water to show the water changing into wine. Be sure to point out that Jesus used power instead of powder!

Note: When you're finished playing with your puppets, remove the tape from them, place them in an envelope, and tape the envelope inside this book so you will have them to play with again and again.

Jesus Fills the Net

Using the code, put a letter in each blank to finish the story. When you're done, enjoy reading the story.

CODE
A=26, B=25, C=24, D=23, E=22, F=21, G=20, H=19, I=18, J=17, K=16, L=15, M=14, N=13, O=12, P=11, Q=10, R=9, S=8, T=7, U=6, V=5, W=4, X=3, Y=2, Z=1

One day __ __ __ __ __ told __ __ __ __ __ to take his __ __ __ __ into deep __ __ __ __ __ and let __ __ __ __ his __ __ __ to a lot of __ __ __ __ . __ __ __ __ __ said, "We __ __ __ __ __ __ all __ __ __ __ __ and didn't __ __ __ __ __ anything, but I'll let __ __ __ __ the __ __ __ again anyway." After he __ __ __ __ __ __ it, the __ __ __ filled up with so many __ __ __ __ that it __ __ __ __ __ . The __ __ __ __ filled two __ __ __ __ __ and the boats began to __ __ __ __ . __ __ __ __ __ __ __ __ __ __ and everyone else were __ __ __ __ __ __ . Simon Peter __ __ __ __ at Jesus' __ __ __ __ __ . Jesus said, "From now on, you will __ __ __ __ __ men." He meant that Simon Peter and his fishing __ __ __ __ __ __ __ __ would __ __ __ __ __ __ __ __ __ __ __ into the __ __ __ __ __ __ __ of __ __ __ .

 Draw a star in this box when you've read the story in Luke 5:3-11.

11

Become a "Fisher of Men"

Jesus wants us to be fishers of men like His disciples. He wants us to tell others about Him so they will want to follow Him, too. Sometimes it's hard to think of ways to tell people about Jesus. Here are a few "hooks" you can use to get your friends interested in talking about Jesus. *As you talk to your friends about Jesus, write their names on the fish.*

Ask your friend if you can tell him or her a story about a miracle.

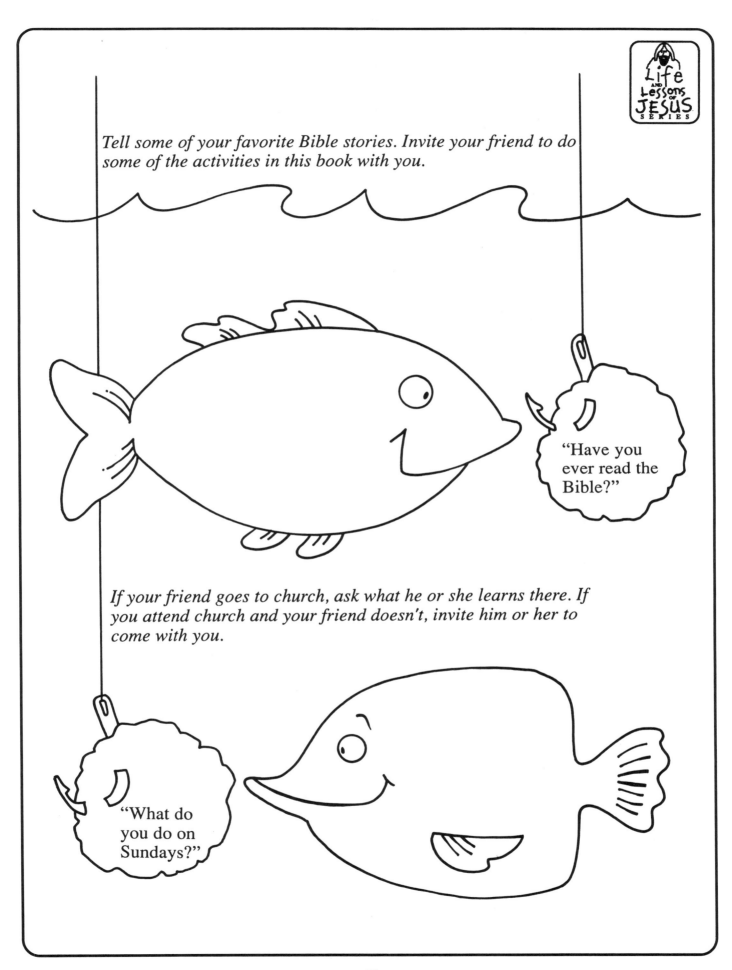

Make a Sponge Fish

Make this fun bath toy for yourself or your younger brothers or sisters to remind you of the miracle of the fish in the nets.

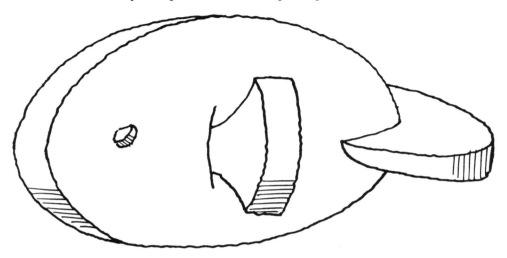

What You Need

- two oval sponges that are different colors
- pencil
- scissors
- a little help from a grown-up

What You Do

1. Use the pencil to poke a hole for the eye in sponge #1. Use the scissors to cut slits in sponge #1 for the two fins.

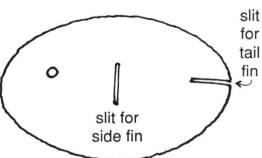

2. Cut sponge #2 into four pieces shaped like these.

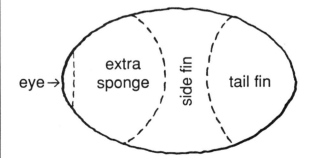

3. Poke the eyepiece cut from sponge #2 into the eyehole on sponge #1. Poke the side fin cut from sponge #2 into the side fin slit on sponge #1. And poke the tail fin cut from sponge #2 through the tail fin slit on sponge #1.

Make a Boat

One day Jesus and His disciples wanted to cross the Sea of Galilee. You can read what happened when Jesus and His disciples crossed the Sea of Galilee in Matthew 8:22-27; Mark 4:35-41; and Luke 8:22-25.

Make this "boat," and pretend your bathtub or a puddle is the Sea of Galilee. When you've read the story, act it out with your boat.

What You Need

- cardboard milk carton
- stapler
- scissors
- piece of clay
- drinking straw
- paper hole punch
- square piece of paper

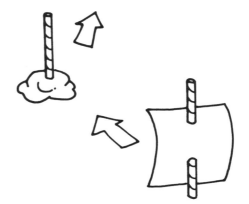

What You Do

1. *Staple the top of the milk carton shut. Then cut out one side of the carton.*

2. *To make the sail, punch two holes on opposite sides of the square of paper. You'll want the holes punched in the center and not too close to the edge. Next, poke the straw through the holes for your sail.*

3. *Place a wad of clay inside the carton, near the stapled top, and stick the straw into the clay so it stands up straight.*

4. *Go float your boat!*

☐ *Draw a star in this box when you've read the story in Matthew 8:23-27; Mark 4:35-41; and Luke 8:22-25.*

Caught in a Storm

The disciples were terrified that they would drown at sea. They woke Jesus and asked Him to save them. Jesus stood up and told the winds and the sea to be calm and still. Immediately, the wind stopped and the sea became calm. *Color this picture.*

Have you ever been caught in a bad storm or another scary situation? *Write about how you felt.*

_____
_____
_____
_____
_____
_____
_____
_____

How would you have felt if you were in the boat with Jesus and the disciples when that storm came up? *Write what you would have done.*

_____
_____
_____
_____
_____
_____
_____
_____

How would you have felt if you saw Jesus calm the storm? *Write what this miracle shows you about Jesus.*

_____
_____
_____
_____
_____
_____
_____
_____

Tossed About in the Storm

While Jesus was sound asleep in the rear part of the ship, a terrible storm arose. The waves crashed over the ship and filled part of it. *Find the ship and ten other items in this storm. Look for a ship, an anchor, a treasure chest, a fish, a sea gull, a fishing pole, a net, a shell, a sandal, a pillow, and a candle.*

See the Sea

Make a sea in a bottle. To show what the sea looked like during the storm while Jesus was asleep, shake the jar. Keep it still to show what happened when Jesus said, "Peace, be still."

What You Need
- small, clean jar with lid
- white vinegar
- blue and green food coloring
- salad oil
- salt

What You Do

1. Fill the jar half full with white vinegar.
2. Add one or two drops of food coloring.
3. Screw on the lid and shake the jar until the food coloring and vinegar are mixed together.
4. Open the jar and add salad oil until the jar is full. Because sea water is salty, you might want to add a teaspoon of salt, too. Close the jar tightly and you have a sea in a bottle.

The Missing Word

The apostles were missing it. Sometimes we don't have it either when we're afraid. But trusting in Jesus makes this stronger. *To find the hidden word, fill in each space with a letter with the color it matches. If a space doesn't have a letter, don't color it.*

G=Green   R=Red   Y=Yellow   P=Purple   O=Orange   B=Blue

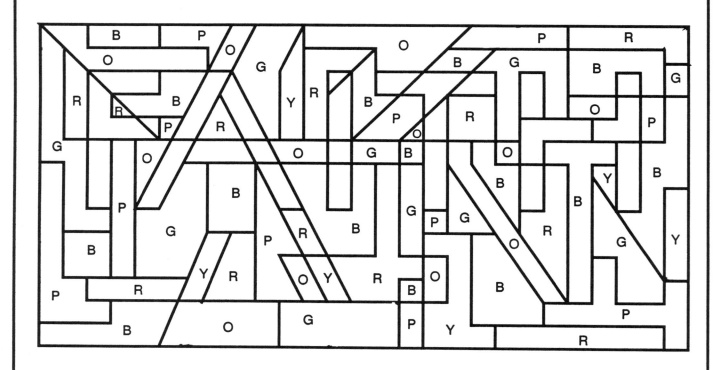

Write the word from the puzzle in the blanks below.

Jesus asked the disciples why they were afraid and why they didn't have more _____. Our _____ grows when we trust the Lord to answer our prayers and ask Him to help us. Then we aren't afraid.

20

A Puzzling Story

Fit each of the underlined words from the story into the puzzle.

One evening Jesus and His disciples needed to cross the SEA of Galilee. A terrible storm AROSE, and the DISCIPLES were AFRAID. They woke up Jesus and asked Him to help them. He performed a MIRACLE. If we have FAITH, the Lord will perform miracles in our lives, too.

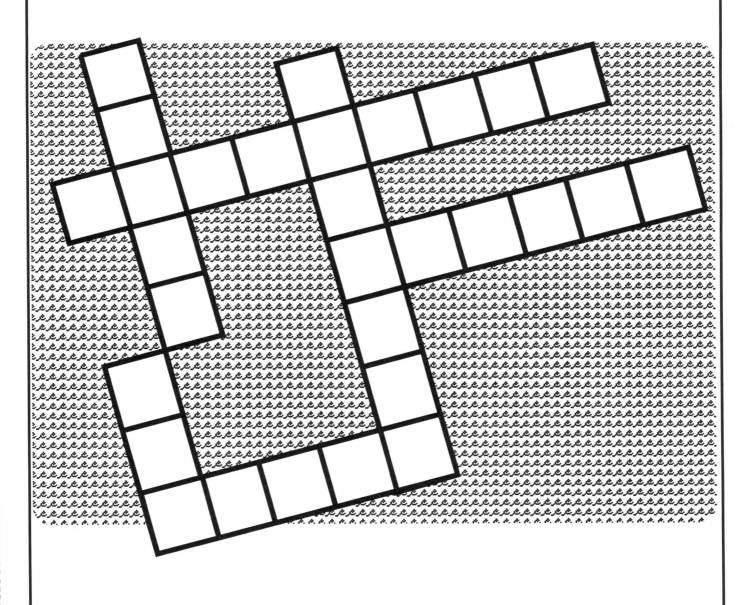

Rely on God

The disciples were amazed when Jesus calmed the storm. They wondered what kind of man would be obeyed by the wind and sea. Jesus had the power to calm the winds and the sea, and He helped His disciples when they were afraid. He can help you, too. *Write down a problem you have or draw a picture, and then write a prayer, asking the Lord to help you with it.*

MY PROBLEM

MY PRAYER FOR THE LORD'S HELP

Jesus Feeds Thousands of People

Finish the story by putting these words in the correct blanks. Use each only once: thanks, desert, loaves, boy, fish, leave, faint, groups, twelve, heaven

One evening after Jesus taught a crowd in the _____, His disciples asked Him to send the people away so they could buy themselves food in the village. Jesus said, "They don't need to _____. You give them something to eat." Andrew said, "There's a young _____ here with five loaves of bread and two small _____, but that's not enough to feed this crowd of people." Jesus said, "Bring the boy to me." Jesus also asked the people to sit on the grass in _____ of fifties and hundreds.

Then Jesus held the five loaves and two fish, looked up to _____, and gave thanks. He gave the bread and fish to the disciples, and they passed out the food to the people. More than 5,000 people were fed that day. Afterward, the disciples picked up _____ baskets of leftovers.

Another time, Jesus had been teaching more than 4,000 people for three days in the wilderness. Now Jesus knew that they were hungry and didn't want to send them away without eating because they might _____. The disciples only had seven _____ of bread and a few fish. Jesus gave _____, divided the bread and fish, and gave them to the disciples, who in turn gave the food to the people. Once again, everyone in the crowd was fed, and this time, there were seven baskets of leftovers.

☐ *Draw a star in this box when you've read these two stories in Matthew 14:15-21; Mark 6:33-44; Luke 9:11-17; John 6:5-15; Matthew 15:32-38; and Mark 8:1-9.*

My 'Loaves and Fish'

Just as God took care of the people's needs, God blesses us every day with food and many other things we need, even though He doesn't usually do it in such an amazing way as in the story you just read. *Write or draw some of the things you're thankful for on the loaves and fish. Remember to thank God for your "loaves and fish" when you pray.*

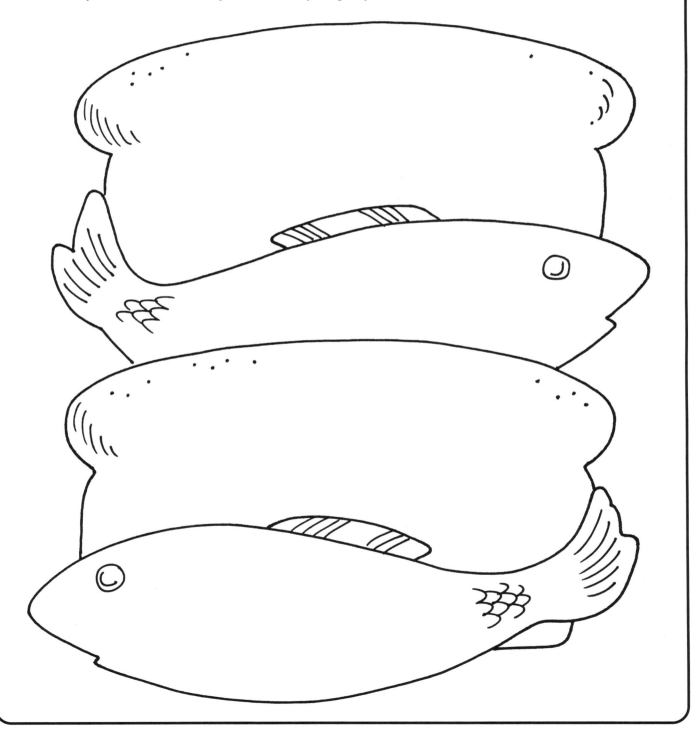

Make a Diorama

Read the story on page 24 again, and then make a diorama (a scene in a box) of Jesus feeding the crowds. With a little imagination and some things from around the house you can recreate the setting of this miracle. The following list of materials and directions are only suggestions to get you thinking.

What You Need

- box
- scissors
- colored paper, Con-Tact paper, or fabric
- glue
- tissue paper
- tape
- pencil
- drawing or construction paper
- paints
- crayons
- dirt, pebbles, or moss
- modeling clay
- foil
- slice of bread

What You Do

1. Cut a rectangular hole on one side of the box. This will be the top of your diorama, and will let in light.

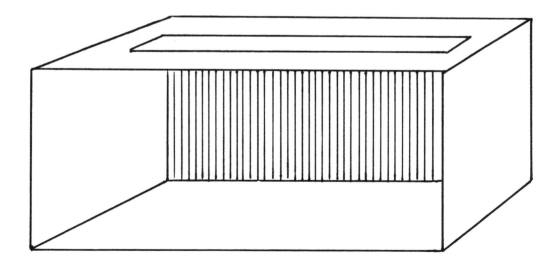

2. Glue colored paper, Con-Tact paper, or fabric to the box, leaving the light hole uncovered. To cover the light hole, tape tissue paper on the inside of the box.
3. Trace the bottom of the box onto a piece of drawing or construction paper. This will make a background for your diorama. Cut out the rectangle, and then paint the scene, draw it, or glue on paper cutouts. Include sky, mountains, people sitting on the grass. Use your imagination and creativity. When you're done with the background, glue it to the back of the diorama.
4. Start making the foreground scene. First, glue dirt, pebbles, moss, or shredded green tissue to the bottom of the diorama.
5. Make figures of Jesus, the disciples, and even the little boy from clay. You could also add fun details like real rocks for the disciples to sit on, baskets, fish made by wadding up tiny pieces of foil, and small pieces of a slice of bread shaped to look like loaves.

Jesus Walks on Water

One day after He finished teaching, Jesus went to the mountains to pray. Meanwhile, His disciples decided to board a ship and cross the sea. While the disciples were at sea, a strong wind blew in and the waves began tossing the ship around.

When Jesus finished praying, it was early morning. Suddenly the disciples saw a figure walking on the water. They were afraid, convinced it was a ghost. Then the figure called out. "Don't be afraid. It's Me, Jesus!"

"Lord," Peter answered, "Lord, if it's really You, ask me to come to You on the water."

Jesus said, "Come."

Peter got out of the ship and, to his amazement, he began to walk on the water toward Jesus. But when Peter noticed how strong the wind was, he was afraid and began to sink. "Lord, save me," Peter shouted. Jesus reached out and caught Peter.

"You don't have much faith. Why did you doubt Me?" Jesus asked.

When they entered the ship, the wind stopped. All the other disciples were amazed and worshiped Jesus. "It's true—You are the Son of God," they said.

After reading this story, number the pictures in the order they belong. The first one is done for you.

Draw a star in this box when you've read the story in Matthew 14:22, 23; Mark 6:45-52; and John 6:17-21.

Would Your Faith Sink or Float?

In tough situations, would your faith in God's help sink or float? *Read each situation, and then check either yes or no. Answer these questions as honestly as you can. Then use your answers for the activity on the next page.*

You're worried about a big test in math. Would you have enough faith to trust God to help you remember what you studied?

YES   NO

Your parents are worried that your old car is going to stop running. Would you have enough faith to trust God to supply a new car or to keep the old one running a little longer?

YES   NO

Your sister is really sick. You've been praying for her for days, but she's not getting any better. Would you have enough faith to trust God to take care of your sister, even when you don't see any answers to your prayer right away?

YES   NO

One of the kids at school got you in trouble with your teacher when you weren't doing anything wrong. Would you have enough faith to trust God to help you forgive him and make things right between the two of you?

YES   NO

Faith to Float

While Peter was walking on the water toward Jesus, he was afraid and began to sink. Do you think you would have trusted Jesus enough to walk to Him on the water? For fun, try this activity.

What You Need

- two clear drinking glasses
- boiled egg
- waterproof marker
- paper
- pencil
- tape
- water
- salt

What You Do

1. Answer the questions on page 30.
2. Draw a face on a boiled egg with a waterproof marker.
3. Fill two clear drinking glasses half full of water. Label one "yes" and the other "no."
4. Add three tablespoons of salt to the "yes" glass and stir until the salt dissolves.
5. Reread each question and gently drop the egg into the cup labeled the way you answered to see whether you would have shown faith or not. This activity is especially fun to do with friends who don't know there is salt in the water. Ask them the questions and drop the egg in the glass for each answer.

Make a String Picture

Read about the miracle of the coin in the fish's mouth on page 35. Then make a string picture using the pattern on page 33.

What You Need

- thin, white, 8 1/2" x 11" piece of cardboard or poster board
- dull needle
- coin or piece of foil
- colored thread or embroidery floss

What You Do

1. Place the fish pattern from page 33 on top of the cardboard.
2. Use a dull needle to punch holes through the dots marked on the pattern.
3. Remove the pattern and glue a coin or circle made of foil to cardboard as shown on the pattern.
4. Sew colored thread or embroidery floss through the holes, following numbers in order on the pattern.
5. When you finish, the cardboard should have threads where there are lines on this pattern.

PATTERN

Do not cut this out, punch holes through it onto the cardboard.

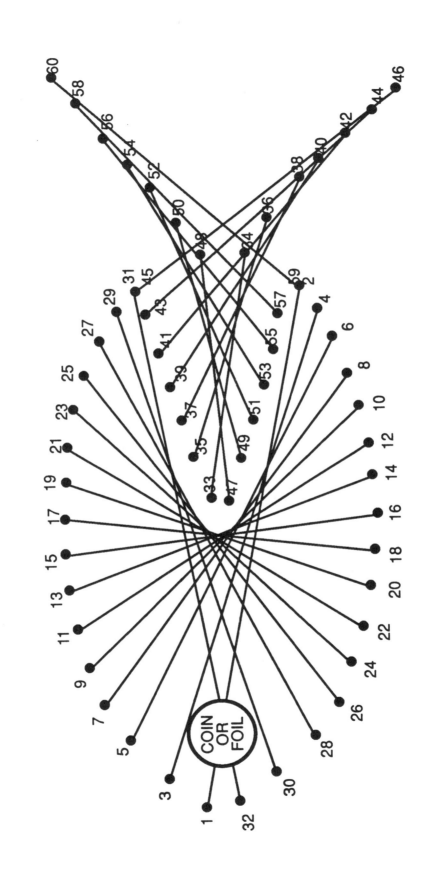

The Coin in a Fish's Mouth

1 day some asked &

2 pay a 4 the .

 told 2  2 the &

2  . told 2 O+

the of the 1st he caught

& there   a N+side.

 Jesus  Peter Temple

Draw a star in this box when you've read the story in Matthew 17:24-27.

Jesus Withers a Fig Tree

Read the story and then find each of the bold words in the puzzle on the next page.

One day **Jesus** was **hungry** and when He saw a **fig tree**, He went to it **hoping** to find **fruit**. There wasn't any, and Jesus said, "Let no fruit **grow** on you from now **on**." The **next** day the tree dried up from its **roots**. The **disciples** (followers of Jesus) marveled and Jesus said to them, "If you have **faith** and do not **doubt**, you will be able to do things like what was **done** to the fig tree, and you will also **say** to this **mountain**, 'Go, throw yourself into the **sea**,' and it will **be** done. If you believe, you will **receive** whatever you **ask** for in **prayer**."

Draw a star in this box when you've read the story in Matthew 21:18-22 and Mark 11:12-14, 20-26.

```
R K J L P N R E Y A R P B Z C R D L
G O M D R K S K M E R I A L K I D P
J R S V B A T H U N G R Y N S P Q V
E P O C D I O M J R K N B C Z L B A
S L J W N B O L Y A S Q I U R F E S
U T P U G H R F R M R P Y T P R L K
S S R E M O V E D S L A G S L U I D
P F S F I G S I T E R C T Y U I E E
A W O V L N Y C S X F D O U B T V L
R I R W E C T E W R O V I R O S I L
J V O X Z F A L H O P I N G T D N E
B E T T I S W O T N V R W F R O G V
W X S R Y E V I E C E R S T S N S R
L O T V E S F R H T I A F E B E N A
H E R K V E L M S Z N I A T N U O M
```

Jesus Fills the Nets Again!

After Jesus died on the cross, He came back to life and visited His disciples several times. One time He appeared at the shore. It was morning and Peter and the other disciples had been fishing all night, but hadn't caught a thing.

From the shore, Jesus asked if they had caught anything. His disciples replied no. Jesus then told them to put their net on the right side of the boat. When they did this, they caught so many fish that they couldn't pull in the net. Instead, they had to drag it behind in a smaller boat.

This miracle may have reminded the disciples of when Jesus first called them "fishers of men." It probably helped them remember the other miracles they had seen Jesus do in the past. *Play this game with a friend to see how well you remember the miracles you learned about in this book.*

What You Need

- fish from page 39
- paper clips
- bowl
- string
- stick
- small magnet
- envelope

What You Do

1. Cut out the fish on page 39 and put a paper clip on each fish. You'll notice that each fish has a miracle written on it. Place each fish facedown in a bowl.

2. Make a fishing pole by tying a string to a stick. Use a magnet for "bait" and tie it to the end of the string.

3. Take turns catching the fish. For every fish a player catches, that person has to tell the story of that miracle in order to get a point.

4. After the last fish has been caught and its story told, add up the points. The player with the most points wins.

5. When you're finished, place the fish in an envelope. Then tape the envelope inside this book so you can play the game another time.

Draw a star in this box when you've read the story in John 21:1-24.

ANSWERS

Page 6   1. Yes; 2. No; 3. No; 4. Yes; 5. Yes; 6. No; 7. Yes

Page 7   1-D   4-F
          2-A   5-C
          3-E   6-B

Page 8   One day Jesus, His disciples (followers), and his **mother** (Mary) attended a **wedding**. After a while, the host ran out of **wine**, and Mary told Jesus. Jesus **asked** what Mary wanted Him to do. Mary didn't **answer** but she told the servants to do whatever Jesus told **them** to do.

    There were six **stone** water pots there, which could hold **twenty** or thirty gallons each. Jesus said to **fill** the pots with **water**, and the servants did. Jesus then told one of the servants to give **some** to the host of the wedding **feast**.

    The wedding host didn't believe the wine he tasted had once been water. He said he was happily surprised that the groom had **saved** the best wine for last.

    Jesus did this first **miracle** in Cana of Galilee and His disciples believed that He was God's Son.

Page 11   One day **Jesus** told **Simon Peter** to take his **boat** into deep **water** and let **down** his **net** to **catch** a lot of **fish**. **Simon Peter** said, "We **fished** all **night** and didn't **catch** anything, but I'll let **down** the **net** again anyway." After he **dropped** it, the **net** filled up with so many **fish** that it **broke**. The **fish** filled two **ships** and the boats began to **sink**. **Simon Peter** and everyone else were **amazed**. Simon Peter **fell** at Jesus' **knees**. Jesus said, "From now on, you will **catch** men." He meant that Simon Peter and his fishing **partners** would **bring people** into the **kingdom** of **God**.

Page 18

ANSWERS

Page 20

Page 21

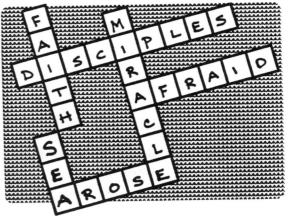

Page 24 One evening after Jesus taught a crowd in the **desert**, His disciples asked Him to send the people away so they could buy themselves food in the village. Jesus said, "They don't need to **leave**. You give them something to eat." Andrew said, "There's a young **boy** here with five loaves of bread and two small **fish**, but that is not enough to feed this crowd of people." Jesus said, "Bring the boy to me." Jesus also asked the people to sit on the grass in **groups** of fifties and hundreds.

Then Jesus held the five loaves and two fish, looked up to **heaven**, and gave thanks. He gave the bread and fish to the disciples, and they passed out the food to the people. More than 5,000 people were fed that day. Afterward, the disciples picked up **twelve** baskets of leftovers.

Another time, Jesus had been teaching more than 4,000 people for three days in the wilderness. Now Jesus knew that they were hungry and didn't want to send them away without eating because they might **faint**. The disciples only had seven **loaves** of bread and a few fish. Jesus gave **thanks**, divided the bread and fish, and gave them to the disciples, who in turn gave the food to the people. Once again, everyone in the crowd was fed, and this time there were seven baskets of leftovers.

Pages 28-29   1-C; 2-F; 3-A; 4-E; 5-D; 6-B

Page 37

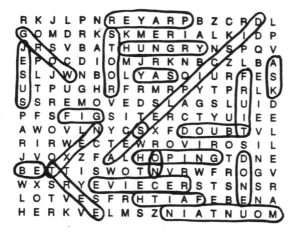

I DID IT!

COMPLETED		DATE	COMPLETED		DATE
☐	Palestine, Where Jesus Lived	_____	☐	A Puzzling Story	_____
☐	Miracles Are A-Maze-ing	_____	☐	Rely on God	_____
☐	Miracle Matchup	_____	☐	Jesus Feeds Thousands	_____
☐	Jesus Changes Water to Wine	_____	☐	My "Loaves and Fish"	_____
☐	Jesus' First Miracle	_____	☐	Make a Diorama	_____
☐	Jesus Fills the Net	_____	☐	Jesus Walks on Water	_____
☐	Become a "Fisher of Men"	_____	☐	Would Your Faith Sink or Float?	_____
☐	Make a Sponge Fish	_____	☐	Faith to Float	_____
☐	Make a Boat	_____	☐	Make a String Picture	_____
☐	Caught in a Storm	_____	☐	The Coin in a Fish's Mouth	_____
☐	Tossed About in a Storm	_____	☐	Jesus Withers a Fig Tree	_____
☐	See the Sea	_____	☐	Jesus Fills the Nets Again!	_____
☐	The Missing Word	_____	☐	Play a Fishing Game	_____

Index of *The Life and Lessons of Jesus* Series

BOOKS
1. Jesus Is Born
2. Jesus Grows Up
3. Jesus Prepares to Serve
4. Jesus Works Miracles
5. Jesus Heals
6. Learning to Love Like Jesus
7. Jesus Teaches Me to Pray
8. Following Jesus
9. Jesus Shows God's Love
10. Names of Jesus
11. Jesus' Last Week
12. Jesus Is Alive!

BIBLE STORY	LIFE AND LESSONS	BIBLE STORY	LIFE AND LESSONS
1st Miraculous Catch of Fish	Book 4	Great Commission	Book 12
2nd Miraculous Catch of Fish	Books 4, 12	Greatest Commandments	Books 6, 8
10 Disciples See Jesus	Book 12	Greatest Is Servant	Book 6
Angels Visit Shepherds	Book 1	Hairs Are Numbered	Book 9
As Father Has Loved Me . . .	Books 9, 11	Hand on Plow	Book 8
Ascension	Book 12	Healing at the Pool of Bethesda	Book 5
Ask in Jesus' Name	Book 11	Healing of 10 Lepers	Book 5
Ask, Seek, Knock	Book 7	Healing of a Blind Man	Book 6
Baby Jesus at the Temple	Book 2	Healing of a Deaf and Mute Man	Book 6
Baptism of Jesus	Book 3	Healing of a Leper	Book 5
Beatitudes	Books 6, 9	Healing of a Man's Hand	Book 5
Becoming Child of God	Book 9	Healing of Blind Bartimaeus	Book 5
Belief and Baptism	Books 8, 12	Healing of Centurion's Servant	Book 5
Blind Leading Blind	Book 8	Healing of Epileptic Boy	Book 5
Boy Jesus at the Temple	Books 2, 3	Healing of Malchus's Ear	Book 5
		Healing of Man Born Blind	Book 6
Calming the Storm	Book 4	Healing of Man with Dropsy	Book 5
Careless Words	Book 6	Healing of Official's Son	Book 5
Christian Christmas Ideas	Book 1	Healing of Peter's Mother-in-Law	Book 5
Christian Easter Story and Activities	Books 11, 12	Healing of the Paralytic	Book 5
Coin in Fish's Mouth	Book 4	Healing of the Woman's Back	Book 5
Count the Cost	Book 8	Healing of Woman Who Touched Hem	Book 5
		Heaven	Book 12
Demons into Pigs	Book 5	How Much God Loves Us	Book 9
Disciples Find a Donkey	Book 11	Humble Prayer	Book 7
Divorce/Stay Married	Book 6		
Do Not Let Your Heart Be Troubled	Book 11	I Am with You Always	Book 12
Don't Insult Others	Book 6	I Live/You Will Live	Book 11
Don't Worry About Food and Clothes	Books 7, 9	Include Others	Book 6
Endure to the End	Book 8	Jesus Clears the Temple	Book 11
Escape to Egypt	Book 2	Jesus Died for Me	Book 9
Extra Mile	Book 6	Jesus Eats with Sinners	Book 9
		Jesus Has Overcome the World	Book 11
Faith of a Mustard Seed	Book 7	Jesus Is 'I AM'	Book 10
Faith to Move a Mountain	Book 7	Jesus Is Arrested	Book 11
Fasting	Book 7	Jesus Is Born	Books 1, 2
Feed My Sheep	Book 12	Jesus Is Buried	Book 11
Feeding the 5,000 and 4,000	Book 4	Jesus Is Christ	Books 3, 10
Forgive	Books 6, 7	Jesus Is Crucified and Dies	Book 11
Forgiven Much, Love Much	Book 9	Jesus Is God	Book 10
		Jesus Is Immanuel	Book 10
		Jesus Is Tempted	Book 3
Gabriel Visits Mary	Book 1	Jesus Is the Bread of Life	Book 10
Garden of Gethsemane	Book 11	Jesus Is the Bridegroom	Book 10
Get Rid of What Causes Sin	Book 8	Jesus Is the Chief Cornerstone	Book 10
Gift of Holy Spirit	Books 9, 12	Jesus Is the Gate	Book 10
Give and Lend	Book 6	Jesus Is the Gift of God	Book 10
Give to Caesar What Is Caesar's	Book 8	Jesus Is the Good Shepherd	Book 10
God and Money	Book 8	Jesus Is the Lamb of God	Book 10
God Gives Good Gifts	Book 7	Jesus Is the Light	Book 10
God Wants Us in Heaven	Book 9	Jesus Is the Redeemer	Book 10
Golden Rule	Book 6	Jesus Is the Resurrection and Life	Book 10
Good Deeds in Secret	Book 8	Jesus Is the Savior	Book 10

Index of *The Life and Lessons of Jesus* Series

BIBLE STORY	LIFE AND LESSONS
Jesus Is the Son of God	Book 10
Jesus Is the Truth	Book 10
Jesus Is the Vine	Book 10
Jesus Is the Way	Books 10, 11
Jesus Is the Word	Book 10
Jesus Loves Children	Book 9
Jesus Obeys Parents	Book 2
Jesus Prayed	Book 7
Jesus Shows Compassion	Book 9
Jesus Washes Disciples' Feet	Books 6, 10, 11
Jesus' Family	Book 2
Jesus' Genealogy	Book 1
Jesus' Trial Before Caiaphas	Book 11
Jesus' Trial Before Pilate	Book 11
John the Baptist	Book 3
Joseph's Dream	Book 1
Judas Betrays Jesus	Books 3, 11
Judge Not	Book 6
Known by Fruits	Book 8
Last Supper	Book 11
Lay Down Life for Friends	Books 8, 10, 11
Lazarus and the Rich Man	Book 8
Life in New Testament Times	Book 2
Light on a Hill	Book 8
Like Days of Noah	Book 12
Like Jonah's Three Days in Fish	Book 12
Lord's Prayer	Book 7
Love Each Other	Book 11
Love Jesus Most	Book 9
Love Me/Obey Me	Book 11
Love One Another	Book 8
Loving Enemies	Books 6, 7
Make Up Quickly	Book 6
Maps of New Testament Times	Books 1-5
Mary and Martha	Book 8
Mary Anoints Jesus with Perfume	Book 11
Mary Visits Elizabeth	Book 1
Name the Baby Jesus	Book 10
Narrow Road	Book 8
New Commandment: Love	Book 6
Nicodemus	Book 8
Not Left As Orphans	Book 11
Old and New Cloth	Book 8
Oxen in a Pit	Book 5
Parable of the Friend at Midnight	Book 7
Parable of the Good Samaritan	Book 6
Parable of the Lost Coin	Book 9
Parable of the Lost Sheep	Book 9
Parable of the Overpaid Workers	Book 8
Parable of the Persistent Widow	Book 7
Parable of the Prodigal Son	Books 7, 8
Parable of the Sheep and Goats	Books 6, 12
Parable of Sower and Seeds	Books 8, 10, 12
Parable of the Ten Young Women	Book 10
Parable of the Unforgiving Servant	Book 6
Parable of Wedding Feast	Book 10
Parable of Weeds	Book 12
Parable of Wise and Foolish Builders	Book 10
Parables of Mustard Seed and Leaven	Books 10, 12
Parables of Treasure, Pearl, Fishnet	Books 10, 12
Passover	Books 2, 10, 11
Peter's Denial	Books 3, 11
Pharisee and Tax Collector at Temple	Book 6
Pharisees' Hypocrisy	Book 8
Pray Always	Book 7
Prepare a Place for You	Books 9, 11, 12
Promise of Holy Spirit	Book 11
Raising of Jairus's Daughter	Book 5
Raising of Lazarus	Book 5
Raising of Widow's Son	Book 5
Rich Toward God	Book 8
Rich Young Ruler	Book 8
Road to Emmaus	Book 12
Salt of the Earth	Book 8
Second Coming	Book 12
Seek Kingdom First	Book 7
Seventy Times Seven	Book 6
Sheep Know His Voice	Book 7
Shepherd Knows Sheep	Book 9
Speck and the Plank	Book 6
Spiritual Harvest	Book 8
Take Up Your Cross	Book 9
Thief in the Night	Book 12
Thomas Sees Resurrected Jesus	Book 12
Transfiguration	Book 3
Treasure in Heaven	Book 8
Triumphal Entry	Book 11
True Members of Jesus' Family	Book 2
Truth Makes You Free	Book 10
Twelve Disciples	Book 3
Two Agree in Prayer	Book 7
Under His Wing	Book 9
Vine and Branches	Book 10
Walking on Water	Book 4
Water to Wine	Book 4
What Makes a Person Unclean	Book 8
Widow's Mites	Book 8
Wine and Wineskins	Book 8
Wise Men Visit Jesus	Book 1
Withered Fig Tree	Book 4
Wolves in Sheep's Clothing	Book 8
Woman at the Well	Book 10
Woman Caught Sinning	Book 6
Worth More than Sparrows	Book 9
Yoke Easy, Burden Light	Book 7
Zaccheus	Book 9

If you would like to write the author, send your letter to:

Your address here

Stamp

Tracy L. Harrast
c/o Church Resources Dept.
David C. Cook Publishing Co.
850 N. Grove Avenue
Elgin, IL 60120